Crate-Training for Your New Puppy

The Best and Easiest Techniques for Crate-Training Your Puppy

By
Linda Welton

The trademarks used are without any consent, and the publication of the trademark is without permission or backing by the trademark owner. All trademarks and brands within this book are for clarifying purposes only and are owned by the owners themselves, not affiliated with this document.

Table of Contents

Introduction

Having a puppy is a big investment of time and money, it's not easy, and it's not cheap. Both you and your family should be aware that the dog will need at least three walks a day, whether it is cold, hot, rainy, or snowy.

In addition to the walks, you have to take care of their education on a constant basis. The education of a puppy is not applied for one week, and that's it; it must be strengthened throughout their life. However, it is true that it is during their first two years of life when we should dedicate more time to them.

A puppy is not a temporary toy for the small children at home, it is a living being that needs care, and that will live an average of ten to fifteen years, some specimens more. So it is a huge responsibility really, think about it well.

At the economic level, it will be necessary to count on the annual veterinary expenses (vaccinations, revisions, anti-parasites) and with your direct cats (food, bed, leashes, toys, knick-knacks).

Chapter 1: Welcome the New Addition in Family

You're all set to get your new puppy home for the very first time! You're overjoyed, but you're still worried that the dog will become reliant on you. "How am I going to teach them?" You may be thinking. Not sure what to feed them? What might we do to save them from ruining the home? How to owe them sufficient time with the hectic schedule? Even if you aren't even concerned about this stuff, you should. It's tempting to get carried away by the joy of getting a new puppy, but don't underestimate the burden that brings with it. But don't be scared! Here we are, pointing the right direction if you did your homework and deliberately selected the best dog for your home, or you got a dog on the spur of the moment and felt like you bit off more than you'll ever chew. That isn't to suggest that getting used to seeing the dog as part of everyday life won't take a bit of time.

Similarly, it will take time for the dog to adjust to his new surroundings. They won't know what's required of them, so you'll need a lot of patience and tolerance for now. You can say things will not go flawlessly, and that's fine! This chapter will assist you with making the shift as painless as possible.

- **The Ride Towards Home**

Bring another individual with you when you pick up your dog on homecoming day so that you can concentrate on the dog whereas the driver concentrates on the drive. Since your dog's protection and health should still come first, a travel carrier, normally made of sturdy plastic, is the best way to carry a dog in a car. If you don't have a crate, sit in the back seat with your puppy on your lap or even in the seat next to you.

Keep your dog on an old sheet or blanket; it's better to cover the car and your clothes if they have a potty incident or become carsick on the drive home. Walk your new dog before the trip and make them clean their bladder, and keep them out a bit. If you're traveling a long distance, you'll need to stop for toilet breaks every hour or so. While an elderly dog would keep on for longer, we recommend always to break every hour or so to let them out from the car, as they may be nervous due to the unexpected switch in the surroundings.

If your new puppy hasn't been properly vaccinated, stay away from places where other dogs congregate, like pet facilities at highway bus stations. Rather, go off the beaten track to places where there aren't many other puppies. During the car ride, your dog can scream or moan, but do not threaten them in any way. Concentrate solely on soothing them and getting them home safely.

- **Reach Home**

When you get there, take it slowly. See it from your dog's point of view: not long ago, dogs were in a different environment, with a completely different situation. Dogs, like people, need some time to adapt. It would help if you took yours for a walk over the front yard, preferably on a leash. However, if you have a little dog, a leash would frighten them, so you can allow them to scurry about as long as you have the full power of where they go.

After a few minutes, take the dog into the house on a leash or in your arms. Allow your dog to get used to the situation at first. For a puppy, everything is different. And if your dog is an adult, this is their first visit to your home. For the time being, confine your dog to an enclosed space, such as the kitchen, which is cordoned off with baby gates to enable them to explore. In the next few days, you'll like to expose them to the entire family progressively. Many people are willing to let their dog run around the house unsupervised, perfect for brief periods. However, people's most common error when they have a new puppy is giving them too much independence too soon. In reality, for the best performance, monitoring your dog's surroundings for the very first six months to a year of training is critical.

1.1 Introduce Family Members

Introduce one new factor at a time before allowing your dog to meet your children and other family pets. Now is not the time to welcome any of your families, colleagues, and neighbors over; instead, focus on your immediate family and keep things quiet. Even be cautious; unexpectedly allowing the dog to play with the family cat can be disastrous in certain cases. It is a procedure that cannot be rushed. Here's how to make all the family introductions run as smoothly as possible:

1. Children Introduction

According to research, more than 4.5 million individuals are attacked by dogs each year, and kids are not just the most common targets but also the most likely to be critically injured. That's why it's crucial to teach children to value a dog's personal space. A dog can be easily agitated by a bit, unpredictable fast-moving, individual, so a child should never annoy a dog while eating or sleeping and should never run over to one.

Of course, when interacting with children, this is better said than done, so you must closely observe any activities among your puppy and kids. Part of it involves assisting the child in making a positive first impact. To continue, maintain control of the situation—you don't want a dog to bring down a baby, and you still don't want a small child to tug on a puppy's tail. Ask your kids to treat the dog with care. When a kid offers the dog a nice reward, such as a chicken piece, many first interactions go well.

It essentially tells the dog, "I'm fine so that you can believe me." Allow the child to throw a chunk of meat to the puppy from a distance of a few feet. When it comes to getting your dog used to a new situation, space is indeed your friend. Plus, juggling the food will help it run more quickly if the puppy can roughly catch rewards. Allow the dog to approach your child rather than allowing your child to drench their new pet and expect the puppy to cope. Look for short, pleasant experiences. Ask your kid to stay seated and gently pat the dog once the dog has completed the reward and seems relaxed.

Also, keep in mind that the dog is your responsibility, even though your child is overjoyed with their new addition to the family. Not really that you shouldn't allow your children to play with and care about the family dog, but you should have reasonable standards. If they're passionate about it, kids more than eleven can start training the family pet, but it's unrealistic to ask the dog to listen to children much smaller than that.

1.2 Essential Procedures

You intend to take the new puppy to the veterinarian once they arrive at the house. Your dog, on the other hand, may have been prodded and poked and even going through surgery before they arrive. Any of these treatments are important for your dog's welfare and well-being, while others are needless and could cause them discomfort. Here's how it works:

1. Select a Vet

Before you bring your dog home, you can stay in contact with a veterinarian. For instance, you don't want to waste time looking for a veterinarian and making a rushed decision when the puppy is in urgent need of veterinary help. Even though a veterinarian examines your new puppy where you find them, and you can have them examined by a veterinary practitioner you trust within 48 hours of taking them home to ensure their safety.

Because of their immature immune systems and the possibility of contracting an infection from several of the other animals they lived with, dogs, particularly those from shelters and puppy shops, usually arrive home with minor illnesses. If the dog develops a cough, the vet will ensure that the necessary medication is administrated before it progresses to pneumonia. If they have a minor eye problem, a veterinarian will cure it before it gets worse. A veterinarian will even tell you if your new dog has some possibly serious health problems that would take more time and resources than you have available. It's best to find out about those issues as quickly as possible so that you can make the tough decision to return the dog if necessary.

To select a veterinarian, ask your dog-owning friends and relatives for advice. If you've narrowed down your choices, visit the veterinarians' offices and see which one is Dr. Perfect. Here are some things to keep an eye out for:

- Check to see if the premises are safe and if the receptionist, supervisors, and other workers are polite and supportive. How can they deal with customers over the phone call? Are they friendly with the animals who come in?

- Determine the number of veterinarians on board. Whether it's a big clinic, find out if the dog will always see the particular vet. Getting multiple veterinarians on board can be advantageous since each one specialized in a different field. If the clinic is tiny, find out who will substitute for the veterinarian if he is on leave or even out of the hospital.

- Inquire about working hours and emergency procedures. Would you have to go to another facility if your puppy, for example, requires medical assistance at three in the morning? When your pet has to spend the night, who can keep an eye on them? Can the veterinarian answer your calls, and if it is, then when? What services do they have, and, if necessary, will they refer you to a specialist?

- Learn about the veterinarian's schooling. The veterinarian should have earned a veterinary medicine degree from a renowned university. They may also have a great deal of experience, specifically with the breed of your dog.

- Take into account the venue. How much are you able to go for routine medical examinations? What if in case of an emergency?

- Ask about the types of billing accepted by the veterinarian's office. Such practitioners will not endorse premiums (i.e., they will not charge the insurance agent on your behalf, like most human health care companies do); however, they will assist you with filling out the application so that the insurance provider will compensate you.

- Schedule an appointment with your veterinarian and ask them any questions you may have about planning for your puppy registration. Would they seem to be well-informed? Are they straightforward with their communication? Are they willing to spend time answering your questions? Are you pleased with their attitude? Do you comply with their general dog-raising philosophy?

- You should still look for another vet if you or your puppy don't get along with one for some reason.

2. Vaccines

Dogs must be protected against various viruses, including distemper, parvovirus and rabies; before a pup heads home, the first combined injection is usually administered at six to seven weeks of age. Make sure you have a proof of vaccine certificate before you bring up your dog so that you can show it to your vet appointment.

3. Microchip Devices

A microchip could save your dog's life. The majority of the thousands of pets who go missing per year cannot find their way back to their owners. Worse, all of those that are discovered are taken to shelter and potentially euthanized. It could not be possible with the use of a microchip. The microchip is a permanent tracking chip about a rice grain size injected between the pet's shoulder blades by a veterinarian. There are no reported adverse effects. The next move is to register your dog with the microchip provider after it has been microchipped. It's easy—all you have to do is add your contact details, as well as pay a small fee. The data is stored in a database. If the pet somehow goes missing and is found, an individual at a veterinarian's office or a shelter will scan the chip and return them to you. If your new puppy hasn't been microchipped yet, remind your vet to do so before taking her home. Remember to call your pet's microchip provider to correct the details anytime you travel or update your phone number.

4. Deworming Treatment

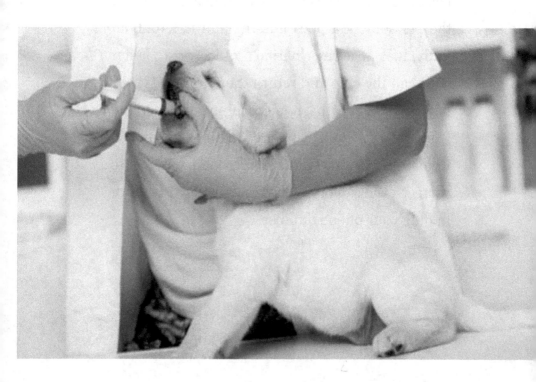

Hookworms, Roundworms, whipworms & tapeworms are pests that most dogs, regardless of where they come from, pick up from their mothers when in utero or nursing. It is natural, but it must be treated because these parasites can cause anemia, bloating, diarrhea, as well as other intestinal problems in your dog.

These kinds of species can be transferred to people by dogs. A vet will usually spray a deworming solvent into a puppy's mouth until it is about two weeks old, killing any parasites. Follow-up procedures will be needed every two weeks before the dog is two to three months old.

5. Ear Cropping and Tail Docking

The deliberate displacement of a portion of a dog's tail is known as tail docking. Ear cropping is the process of removing and forming an animal's earflap to make it stand upright. When performed purely for aesthetic reasons, the American Veterinary Medical Association condemns these practices and "encourages the omission of tail docking and ear cropping from standards."

Tail docking is commonly performed without anesthesia a few days after birth, particularly on some breeds like terriers and spaniels. Surgical knives are used to slit the tails, and the tissue covering them is sewn up. This treatment is unpleasant and may have a long-term impact on how a pup considers pain. Ear cropping is normally performed under local anesthesia on puppies aged eight to twelve weeks. The dog's ears are trimmed and stitched so that they point straight up. Most countries consider these operations to be unconstitutional, but they are nevertheless carried out in few countries. You may not have any choice about whether your puppy's tail is docked or the ears are clipped because, by the time you spot them, the damages may already be done.

6. Removal of Dewclaws

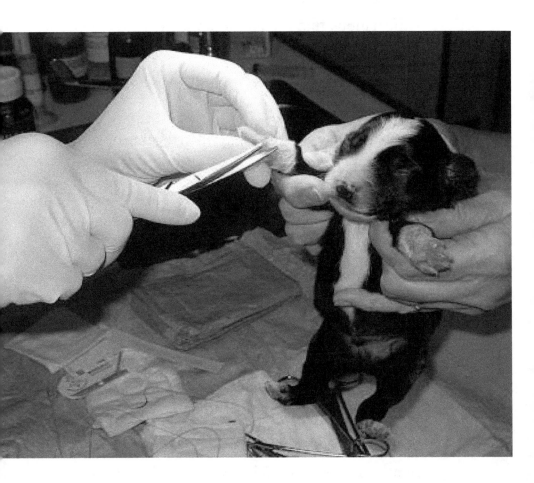

Few dogs are bred with a dewclaw, an additional toe that extends up to the ankle and functions similarly to a human thumb. Apart from ear cropping or tail docking, there are certain medical explanations that a puppy's dewclaws should be cut.

Dewclaws may get frustrated when digging or get stuck on barriers or carpets, or a puppy can bang them against surfaces while running around the house. When a puppy is a newborn, the dewclaws are often cut by breeders. You can have them out later by your veterinarian, but the quicker, the better.

7. Neutering or Spaying

It's no mystery that preventing your dog from reproducing is critical (unless you're a fully skilled licensed breeder). Spaying a female dog means removing her reproductive organs, uterus, fallopian tubes, while neutering a male dog means removing his testicles. It aims to combat dog overpopulation: every year, millions of stray dogs reach shelters, with many being euthanized. That being said, it's still a contentious issue, and many misconceptions about such procedures remain. To clarify the situation on a couple of them, spayed or neutered dogs are never more likely to gain weight, and male dogs will not have identification issues due to losing their "masculinity." Quite enough food and little exercise allow dogs to gain weight, and there's no reason to believe that puppies identify with their sex in the same way that humans do. There are no doubt surgical and anesthetic risks for any medical operation, but the probability of infection is very limited. These surgeries provide the dog with several valuable advantages: Female dogs who are spayed are less likely to experience breast, uterine, or ovarian cancer in life ahead, while neutered male dogs are less likely to develop prostate and penile tumors, along with other health issues.

Additionally, hormone-related behavioral problems such as scent tagging, wandering, and humping can be minimized. When is the safest time to get your pet spayed or neutered? Before the first heat period or before six months of age in females; and before eight months of age in males. Consult your veterinarian on the best possible time for your dog.

8. Call for a Name

Try involving the entire family in this enjoyable step. Do it cautiously all; you'll be hearing the dog's name hundreds of times per day! You may have learned that if a dog's name resonates with words such as "sit," "come," or "gone," they will get quickly confused. Dogs are intelligent and capable of distinguishing between different things, as you'll discover as you read this book.

Others might suggest that a name be shorter, while others will recommend against giving the dog a human name since it might humanize them. These viewpoints are much too prevalent for dogs and are simply untrue. You should use your sound knowledge for selecting a name. A name as Juggernaut is a big load, while Sourpuss is obnoxious and has no regard for a puppy. Choose a name for your amazing new pet that is cool, interesting, romantic, nostalgic, or just any name you want.

9. Get Your Family Ready

When a puppy eventually arrives at their new home, their life will seem to be flipped upturned. If you appear to have things in place, they'll be even more at ease. Now is the time to establish certain rules and boundaries and ensure that everybody in your home understands them. There's a clear link between consistency and the outcomes you can predict! If you, your partner, children, friend, or someone else who may have a lot of interaction with your dog is inconsistent, your dog will not learn who to respond to and who to neglect. Find the following:

- Remember to keep your dog's well-being in mind at all times. Whether you have a pup or a little dog, instruct your children to never leave them on a sofa or table where they might collapse and injure themselves badly. Permit small children to carry them only when they are seated. Never leave a young child alone with a pup.

- Warn everybody in the house that the puppy can chew on anything that can get their hands on. If the kids come home from school and dump the bags on the floor, the dog can smell their unfinished lunch or other "food items." Also, inform them that their pet can damage and choke on their belongings, such as figurines and plush toys. At first, you can't trust them to be able to distinguish between other toys and theirs.

- Choose a family member to be the dog's primary coach. Then, if the person has a better understanding of the family dog's unique personality and how to deal with them successfully, they will show the entire family how to do it. This way, the dog will have the main trainer, and the rest of the family should be at the same pace.

Clarify to kids that the dog will take more time to adapt to the new environment; of course, everybody will have lots of chances to play with their new puppy, but they should be aware that she will require some alone time. Be sure; your children aren't harsh on your puppy.

1.3 Grooming

Grooming is an important way to care for your dog, and it varies a lot based on your dog's hair, age, and where you live. Here's a quick rundown:

1. The Very first Bath

You want to embrace your new puppy, but what if they're soaked in piss and feces! Some dogs don't get baths until they're three months old or more, so you can bathe them if that one is filthy. It is, indeed, critical to understanding how to go about it correctly. Often, avoid bathing the dog too much since this will remove moisture and natural oils from their hair and skin. Most sources recommend washing dogs frequently, although others recommend bathing them less often, like as once a month.

It is solely a matter of personal choice and lifestyle—for example, if the dog sleeps in your bed with you, you'll want to make sure they are clean and free of dirt. You should bath your dog in a normal bathtub or a small compact bathtub; some people shower with their pets! The trick is to avoid getting water or soap in your dog's ears, eyes, or nose and avoid just pouring water on their head.

To be extra cautious, you may carefully place cotton balls between your dog's ears. Often, only use gentle shampoos made especially for dogs; consult your veterinarian or groomer to find out that one is better for the dog finally, if you give your frequent dog baths like once a week. Ensure the skin doesn't get dry or flaky, as this might indicate that it's dried out; if this happens, then reduce the number of baths they get or use a moisturizing shampoo to maintain their skin smooth.

2. Nails

It's vital to maintain the dog's nails as short as possible. They might scrape you and your belongings, as well as a scratch on the carpet, and find it harder for the puppy to walk. Conversely, cutting it perfectly can be difficult—cutting them so deeply can cause a great deal of pain and bleed to your puppy.

Ask the groomer or vet to teach you how to do it properly if you intend to do it yourself. Teach your dog a positive relationship for getting their nails clipped until you've learned the correct technique. For instance, show them the nail cutter and sniff it before bringing the nail clipper to the nail. Take it slowly! When your dog acts peacefully, reward them for each little move, eventually leading up to becoming able to trim the nail. In no time, they'll be able to handle having their nails cut!

3. Teeth

We are all aware of the importance of brushing our teeth. What makes you think dogs are any dissimilar? Brush the dog's teeth at least once a day. It not only keeps the breath fresh, but it also helps to stop gum disease, which is widespread in dogs and has been linked to serious diseases like heart, liver, and kidney disease when left untreated. A dog toothbrush or a finger brush can be purchased at a pet supplies shop.

Human toothpaste uses high-foaming cleaning products that a dog might ingest or inhale as they don't know how to spit it out. Instead, try a variety of dog toothpaste flavors once you find one that your dog enjoys. Be sure your dog has more than enough dental snacks and plush toys to chew on, and also high-quality food—some "dental foods" contain plaque—and tartar-reduction additives. Consult your veterinarian on the right diet and treats for your puppy, taking into account the oral and other health requirements. Ask your veterinarian about plaque and tartar preventive care options for eliminating periodontal disease,

If you find oral disease symptoms like weak or discolored teeth, poor breath, bleeding or inflammation in the mouth, drooling, losing food, or a reduced appetite or weight, call the vet. Your vet can check your dog's mouth at their medical exams—or every vet appointment, for such a matter to ensure it appears well.

4. Eyes

It's important to look at your dog's eyes daily to communicate with them. If you notice some gunk residue in the edges, clean it away with a wet cotton ball. Be sure the dog's fur doesn't get in their eyes, as this can irritate. If you notice redness, discoloration, abnormal discharge, swelling, squinting, or a noticeable third eyelid, call the veterinarian. If the pup has rusty tearstains at the edge of their eyes, which are more apparent in white dogs, see the vet check out allergies or tear duct problems. If the stains worry you, speak to your veterinarian about other options—for example, pet supplies shops have items you can spray on your dog's food to help clean up the stain.

5. Ears

Cotton balls and a cleaning solution are used to clean your dog's ears, which can be done at least once a week. Hold the outside of the earflap, then make your way into the ear with a new cotton ball, stopping if you encounter resistance. If the cotton balls get dirty, it may be a symptom of an allergic reaction, so rush the dog to the vet for a checkup. Discharge, crusting, an odor in the ear, redness, and swelling are also symptoms of an infection.

Often, if your dog is itching or rubbing their ear on the floors or other areas, or if they seem to be off-balance, book an appointment to help ensure everything is good. They may be infected with ear mites, a bacterial infection that causes ear inflammation and pain.

6. Hairs or Coat

Some dogs ought to be brushed daily to evade matting and unnecessary shedding, while others need to be brushed once every week, maybe less often. It's critical to use the right brushes and comb; the veterinarian or a licensed groomer will advise you. A slicker comb and a bristle brush may be required for long-haired dogs, while a bristle brush and a plastic brush may be required for dogs with a soft, short coat.

You'll notice that although some dogs like being brushed, some despise it. If the dog belongs to the latter group, take it gently. Allow the dog to smell the brush first, then softly stroke them with it, and finally combing her with the brush gently. Check for lice, pest dirt, bugs, any wounds, sore areas, or any skin conditions that could need medical treatment when grooming your dog. Always remember to be patient!

1.4 Introduce the Leashes

If you haven't done so before, since the dog is already home after a day or two, expose them to the leash. If you have an adult dog, they're probably used to living with a leash; but, if the puppy or dog isn't used to it, they might panic if he senses any strain on it. Take a look at things through their eyes. They've never been restrained or constrained like this before, so it must be strange for them. That's why we need to take constructive steps to help our dog get to know this new product. It is how you can do it.

1. Allow the dog a minute to sniff and investigate the leash—you can keep it or drop it on the floor. The goal is to notify dogs of the presence of a new entity in the house that they must become acquainted with. To help develop a healthy relationship with the leash, bringing out the rewards at this point. We

want them to understand that it will be accompanied by fantastic things if the leash is released.

2. So, while in your sitting room or a similar place, clip the leash to the dog's collar or harness and bring them for a stroll. At first, refrain from grabbing the leash or creating any tension. It's best if we adjust to fewer factors. Initially, the dog might assume the leash as a toy, catch it, and play around with it. Though we'll eventually fix this behavior, it's essential for now that the dog is happy.

3. Make a happy sound or use a high-pitched voice after the dog has walked around with the leash trailing behind them for a while. As a thank you, offer them a treat. Then, very slowly, grab the leash for a second, being careful not to tangle it. Return it to the floor and reward

your dog with a treat, as if to tell, "I like how you handled the first test." Almost all of your dog's training will revolve around this theme. It may sound dumb, to begin with, such a small move, but your dog can learn much more quickly if you get good at cutting stuff down into small steps.

4. Steadily increase the amount of time you carry the leash, praising gently all along the way, as is often the case when teaching new approaches. When your dog is defying or panicking, don't get discouraged. That's your signal to take it slowly for a moment.

5. Finally, practice keeping the chain in one hand while tempting the dog to chase you across the house with treats kept in the other hand. If your dog gets a blast of excitement that creates tension on the leash but does

not panic, promptly rejoice and praise with an extra treat. If they begin to panic, quickly let go of the chain and allow them to walk to you and repeat the procedure. It's fine if your dog needs a few days to get used to walking on a leash; several dogs need more patience.

1.5 It's the Bedtime

When it's time to go to bed, that first exciting day will easily turn awful. When pup waking you up at 4 a.m., the cute little dog doesn't sound so charming. You may even get fortunate and get a dog that sleeps through all the night, but really don't set your hopes too high and don't expect a full night's sleep immediately. In reality, if you have a puppy, you'll probably have to get up once or twice during the few weeks to take them outside.

Don't worry; once the dog has learned, you'll be able to sleep soundly together. However, getting the dog on a timetable will take a few weeks, so be positive. From the time puppies are about 12 weeks old, most of them will sleep all night (approximately eight hours). Your dog could be afraid, alone, and out of control on the first night. It may be a puppy's first time being separated from their siblings and mum. Whether you want your dog to sleep in your bed all the time or not, it's generally a good idea to start them out during the first few days. They'll require some consolation.

A dog crib beside your bed would be your best option. If your dog is afraid of the crib at first and you haven't had them accustomed to it during the daytime, they won't be content sleeping in it at night. Another choice is to place some old clothes or blankets next to your bed and secure their chain to either bed or nightstand securely. In any case, give your pet age-appropriate activity during the day so that they are less tired and more able to relax at night. If your dog screams or whines in the middle of the night, ignore them initially.

Don't grab them up immediately; doing so will encourage them that crying will get them a "step out from the crib and play" reaction. It's fine to let the dog out and briefly comfort them if they've been whining for 20 minutes or more and you've already taken them out. Please don't do this all the time, only for the first few days when the pup is getting used to it. Many lose faith once it comes to sleeping time, so please don't. In this way, getting a new puppy is similar to getting a new newborn. Be understanding of what the dog has been through. You must make them feel at ease and secure. It's a promise that before you know it, the dog (and you!) would be sleeping through the night.

1.6 Feed the Puppy

If at all feasible, hold off on transitioning to a different diet for a few days or weeks. Your dog has enough transitions to cope with now! When you're about to make the transition, though, do it slowly to prevent gastrointestinal issues like diarrhea. Fill one-quarter of the container with new food and three-quarters with old food for three days. The bowl could then be cut in two for the next three days, half with the new food and half with the former. Finally, serve three-quarters

of the new food and one-quarter of the old food for
a few days.

1.7 Social Awareness

Among the most significant things we could do
with the dog is socialize them, particularly
because it can help avoid behavioral issues later
on. The socialization period, which is an
important part of a dog's life, lasts around six to
fourteen weeks. "Throughout that time, favorable
encounters with other pets, humans, sounds, and
movements will decrease the risk of fearful
behaviors, such as hostility and phobias, later in
the dog's life."

Dogs who haven't been adequately socialized are
most likely to have behavioral disorders, which
are the leading cause of dogs being surrendered to
shelter. It's crucial to introduce your dog to
various humans, creatures, environments, smells,
and environments, particularly throughout those
crucial weeks. Continue doing so for the first year
of the dog's life. Take your puppy with you
wherever possible while you're out and around,
and generously compliment them whenever they

are in a different environment or with a new animal or human. (A few morsels of food and other treats wouldn't harm, either!)

Acceptance would be ingrained in pupas as a result of this. Don't panic if you've got an elderly dog; it has been observed that dogs of all ages thrive from socialization. However, it can take you longer and require more patience from your side. There are no easy remedies in certain situations where the dog has experienced extremely limited socialization and has highly rooted negative traits. It can take months, if not years, to make a significant change on these problems, but aim for gradual improvements over time. If the dog also exhibits threatening behavior, such as bared teeth or a desire to strike, withdraw them from the situation, people, or animals immediately. Overall, it's essential to have a healthy relationship when introducing the dog to new species, people, or situations. Here's how you can do it:

1. Different Dogs

We ought to educate our dogs that they aren't the only ones on the planet. They must become used to being around dogs of all sizes and shapes, so they're not afraid, hostile, or even both once they experience them later in life. Many people mistakenly believe that only because the pup gets along with the dog next door and the other pets in the home is socialization. Take into consideration this from a human standpoint: only because you get along with your closest mate, siblings, and parents doesn't guarantee you'll get along with anyone else. That's something you'll have to reflect on.

Consider this: if that were the only individuals you spent time with, you'd certainly behave differently around outsiders. It's important to concentrate on socializing your canine with all other pleasant dogs. You don't want the dog to come across some other dog that growls at them or threatens to hurt them. So, if you know someone who has a dog you'd like to meet, inquire about how the dog plays with other dogs. Go on gently whether the individual is reluctant or says something more than, "They like other dogs!" If far as possible, leave out possible negative situations. Your dog would have plenty of opportunities to socialize with other dogs. Now is not the time to drive your puppy to a dog park, then let them race about uninhibitedly.

For one thing, they might easily come across an unfriendly dog and have a bad experience. It is a very normal occurrence at dog parks. Your puppy, make sure it is always with stable, vaccinated dogs to avoid contracting a serious disease. Keep an eye on the dogs' body language: if they're smelling each other and wagging the tails, they're likely to want to play. Whether or both dogs do the "play bow," which involves kneeling on their front legs with their butts in the air (a universal canine invitation to play), it's normally a good indication that situations are going better. Get another dog for yours to socialize with if you notice any unnecessary growling or snapping, or if the dog have their tail among their legs and are afraid or hostile in any way.

2. Different People

It's crucial to introduce your dog to people of all ages, genders, and races, as well as people who seem to be distinctive in some way (from a person in a costume, such as a postman, to somebody with a beard or anyone who uses a walker or pushchair). To avoid upsetting your dog, consider having on a huge hat and shades and opening your umbrella from a safe distance—these are all things they might find unsettling if he isn't used to them.

Don't forget to introduce your dog to many men. Due to their broad body shapes or heavy voices, dogs may find men frightening. It can take a dog from week to months to generalize like that. It was, indeed, a beginning—select people who can treat the pet respectfully and guarantee that they have a good experience. Kids, who may be inadvertently rough, must be avoided throughout all times. Bring healthy treats with you whenever you're socializing your puppy and motivate others to do the same. Presuming the dog responds well, have someone gently stroke them under the chin rather than on the head. It makes them understand that people need not be frightened.

3. Routine Life Experiences

Together with socializing your dog with other animals and humans, it's important to make them feel at ease in various situations, from commuting to experiencing sirens to encountering a blow dryer, stairwells, a washing machine, or even popcorn popping in the microwave. Allow them to observe bikes, road workers, and leaf blowers.

The more sights, sounds, and observations the dog has, the easier. The trick is to take it slowly and break up new interactions into small parts, particularly if your dog is hesitant. For example, if you're using a washing machine, let the dog sniff it first (while it's turned off, obvious). Then, please turn it on and demonstrate to the dog that it makes a sound for a brief moment. If all goes well, progressively raise the time, you have the machine running, and take a moment if your dog seems to be scared. Every step of the way, give your dog a treat and praise them.

Chapter 2: Crate

Training

Your dog's crate is their haven, a spot where they can get aside from everything. They sleep there at night and are contained there sometime during the daytime. The crate should be your dog's sanctuary rather than a crate, which should be correlated with praise instead of a penalty. Since most dogs prefer a comfortable room space, the crate is not present in nature, so usually, puppies should be taught to enjoy their crate. The most important argument to crate trains the dog would be that crate-trained puppies are usually well trained in particular.

Crating leads a puppy to relax and enjoy some alone time. Since you offer dogs specific stuff when they are in the crate, it allows them to bite on suitable objects. Crate-trained dogs are more capable of coping with fear and, if required, resettling. A dog's crate ensures security and warmth while they travel. Dealing with crate-trained puppies is a joy for veterinarians and groomers, and you will enjoy it too.

Crate train the pup even though you work from home. Using a crate is close to using a baby's playpen or an infant's crib: It offers a secure room where you can look away from your child for a few minutes. Never allow your dog to get unaccustomed to being crateed. A crate-trained dog is expected to spend more time within the crate than anywhere else in their life, so it's essential to keep it secure and safe.

Your dog's bed or rug must have a washable sheet, should be placed in the crate. Often dogs prefer to curl up against a padded surface or bolster. Since some people associate crate training with potty training, it's necessary to explain that the crate is not your dog's toilet. Although good crate training helps with toilet training, never use the dog's crate as their toilet if you plan on making the puppy poop within your house. Arrange a pan next to the crate for the puppy's potty needs instead.

2.1 Reasons for Crate Training

Most people object to the concept of confining a creature, particularly a cherished and loving pet, in a "crate." Besides, the majority of dog lovers consider their dogs to be personal companions. As no one will even put their best mate, infant, or toddler in a crate, confining a dog in one could seem barbaric. Conversely, if puppies are well-coded and have a good mindset, they will tolerate or even enjoy their leisure time alone.

The crate is made for the dog's safety as well as the owner's ease and peace. A crate, for instance, keeps a dog safe from the contaminants under the dishwasher, provides a peaceful spot for them to relax while they are sick, and makes them safe on car rides. A correctly crate-trained puppy will deem the crate to be "their" room and visit it when they choose.

Crate teaching succeeds since dogs enjoy a safe and private sleeping space. Dogs, as their prehistoric relatives, want a secure "shed" to call home. Even though we tend to assume that our puppies are quite human, they all have wolf tendencies. Understanding our dogs' intuition is essential to make them feel protected, comfortable, and content in the homes. Crate training is an essential aspect of incorporating puppies into our worlds and establishing a trusting relationship between humans and dogs.

2.2 Dos and Don'ts of Crate Training

Crate training will begin as early as eight to twelve weeks of age for puppies. Their mother has been keeping their "place" spotless, so they are used to sleeping in a tidy space. Since puppies have less bladder control and require more regular potty visits, crate training a puppy can be a little longer and more effort than crate training an adult dog.

Read through these dos and don'ts before beginning your puppy's training:

- No matter how angry you are when the pup screws up, never put them in the crate as a penalty.

- Provide no food or drink in the crate until the pet is fully housebroken.

- Crating after a meal is never a good idea, no matter how old they are. Constipation, an inflammation of the stomach that can be fatal, can occur if a dog does not drink enough water or work out.

- Do not limit the amount of water the dog consumes throughout the day, and ensure regularly scheduled visits to the potty zone, particularly for puppies.

- Understand your dog's urinary control issues. Puppies don't fully develop bladder control until they're around six months old.

- In any case, avoid keeping your crateed dog unmonitored in any place where the sun will shine on the crate (like a car, garden, or house). In the sun, crates become frying cookers. Dogs with thick or darkened fur, tiny whiskers, or light fur are especially vulnerable to hot weather.

- Take off the dog's leash before putting them in the crate. A dog's leash may get tangled in the gate or other internal components, which can be choking them.

- Please make sure the bedding and toys you put in the dog's crate are appropriate for them. Toys that are tiny enough to be eaten or clunky enough to be chewed into tiny chunks can trigger choking and gastrointestinal issues.

- Teach children (whether members of your family or guests) that perhaps the crate is out of their limit at all moments. Whether or not they are in it, the crate is the dog's personal space.

- Allowing other family pets into the dog's crate or bothering the dog when they are inside is not a good idea.

2.3 Benefits of Crate Training

Crate preparation is an essential component of your puppy's ongoing training for a variety of reasons. Here we discuss your dog as a pup as that's when crate training probably begins. In several cases, the guidelines extend to an adult dog as well. However, older dogs usually are quicker to crate-train, unlike puppies; using a crate will assist with the following:

- House training a dog.

- Enable traveling a secure experience.

- Discourage unhealthy habits.

- Allow the pup to have his room.

- Keep a dog out of harm's way.

- Keeping a sick pup in a crate is a good idea.

- Give Time out the dog.

Let's take a deep look at above mention points.

1. House Training

A puppy's innate nature is to protect its "space." If you intend to keep your dog at home along with you, then you must reap the benefits of this tendency for house training. A tiny space, like a restroom or washing area, is also too massive for a puppy's "clean house" intuition to kick in. When a dog is trapped in the shower, it is likely to ease itself on one end and nap on the other. However, if the dog is held in an appropriately fitted crate, they would most certainly "bear it" until brought outside.

2. Travel Security

As your puppy can mess with the traveling, a crate is a healthy way to limit them when you ride them in the car. Whenever you need to go out of the car for a while, the crate encourages you to open the windows for rest without the dog getting out or messing with people on the street. (Obviously, ensure you park in the canopy.) Whenever you need to drop the dog at the vet's clinic, a rehabilitation crate, or a mate's place, their crate may help them cope with the separation anxiety they can experience.

They'll have their own compact "room," which will act as a haven. When you take your dog on holiday, several guesthouses and resorts will accept crate-trained dogs so they cannot ruin the space if they have been contained. Most people house their pets in cordoned crates in the back of their cars. A crate accomplishes the same goal, but it is also compact and provides the dog with a secure, friendly, and soothing atmosphere.

3. Let Rid of Negative Habits

A pup should not walk freely in the home until it has been adequately conditioned for the animal's protection and your belongings. The puppy can meet poisonous plants, domestic chemicals, fans, electric cables, drugs, and other potentially hazardous things. They might make sparklers out of Sunday newspapers or might chew on your beloved shoes or the leg of the vintage chair. It's impossible to break poor biting, scratching, and ripping habits once they've begun. If you're out of home, keep the puppy restricted with some toys, and tell them which objects are "reasonable" when you're back, and the puppy is free.

4. Allowing the Puppy to Have Some Privacy

A dog will soon and cheerfully realize that the crate is theirs. Its dogs own space where they can go when sleepy or irritable. They may hold their beloved toy or chewing object there regardless of being disturbed by the pet cat or some other dog. If you have disobedient children or a buddy's unpleasant pet coming, the crate offers a safe space for the puppy.

In these cases, the puppy will go to the crate on its own. You might want to put a snack in the crate for them to relax without being distracted by the guest. If the crate is made up of wire, you should cover it with a cloth to maintain protection during the visit; if guest children are inclined to peek inside the crate, gently remind them that the puppy is asleep and shouldn't be interrupted.

5. Location Flexibility

When you don't like dog fur on the bed or puppy snores beside your ears, a bedroom crate will encourage the puppy to connect to you; the group alpha is in the room despite having to sleep on the bed. This agreement would provide them with the comfort of sleeping "with the pack" while not violating your specific sleeping room.

They can also be secure in the pantry while you cut vegetables for lunch or in the driveway while replacing the antifreeze in the car. (Dogs are killed by antifreeze!) Although your puppy would also need housebreaking and family manners instruction, using a crate will help you establish a feeling of caring love, and affection with a stubborn and sly dog as he develops appropriate conduct.

6. Convalescence Is a Stable Atmosphere

When your dog needs to be contained due to sickness or accident, a crate can help tremendously. It could be a personal, comfortable, and secure environment whereby the puppy can recover, free from other pets and even children's interference.

7. Time-Out Location

A puppy's conduct is usually hyperactive. If a game or a long walk doesn't succeed, you can channel your dog's energy by offering the pup a treat and putting it in the crate. When the dog is placed in the crate, never let the pup feel being abused or exiled. With gentle and inspiring terms, lead them into the crate and give them one or any of their favorite treats.

2.4 Variety of Crates

Crates, commonly known as crates, are available in a wide range of sizes and materials. The dog's height, age will determine the style you select and breed your cost estimate; and whether you want to commute with your pet (by road or by air). Long-term isolation cannot be done by crate conditioning. Adult dogs that have been well conditioned and are in good shape will generally sit in the crate for up to 9 hours. Don't keep the dog in the crate for much longer.

Furthermore, the crate should not be used as a means of punishment. If you use the crate for extended periods or as a penalty, the puppy can develop various depression habits that are unsafe for the puppy, upsetting for you, and stressful for both of you. Crate sizes range from tiny ones for a little Chihuahua to those big ones for a German Shepherd, depending on the maker. Many crates are simple, and others are ornate.

There are also crates of wired walls that resemble small doghouses. What design you choose, ensure the construction and materials are of good quality. All crates worsen with time, based on use; however, with proper care, they will last for ten years or more.

1. Crates for Flying by Plane

Several companies produce crates designed especially for air transport, and they vary in quality from average to plush. Differences are based on the colors and styles of gates, ventilation, and seals. The price varies from around $20 to almost $200. Every crate is divided into two rigid plastic parts (upper part and lower part) and a wire gate on its front. Bolts are used to bind the upper and lower parts. Steel walls with drilled holes in the plastic would cover the ventilation gaps on either top right half. The back of one brand's crate even has vent holes. Silver, plastic-coated aluminum, or plastic are used to building the wire door.

A few of the small crates might have a carrying hook on the top. Crates for air transport are generally made of hardened plastics with the front fender and ventilation from both sides. They make stable and comfortable dens for roaming puppies or dogs who are typically restless or hyperactive as they provide pretty enough security from the outside surrounding. A crate built for air transport is easy to clean and disinfect, provides optimum confidentiality and is relatively light.

However, it is more a little cross vent than a wire crate, so its positioning in the house must be thoroughly thought.

As heat persistence is higher in this form of crate than in a wire crate, it's not the safest option for dogs with thick fur. Any air transport crate' floors aren't completely level and could have elevated and incised sections. Pick a crate with an utterly level bottom. If you can't search one, cut a plywood sheet underneath the mat to give your dog a much more stable surface.

2. Crates Made of Solid Wire

Rigid-wire crates are available in various materials, including chrome plating, galvanizing, painting, and a rubber-type covering. A sturdy metal floor can be seen on the majority of these crates. Few puppies have a predisposition to chew the wire, which has sparked fears about galvanized metal quality in recent years. The cost of such crates ranges from $40 to $130.

A rigid-wire crate requires almost 100% of its total airflow area, but it gives the dog little privacy compared to air travel crates. Few airlines allow wire crates for transporting puppies, but the transparent style lacks tactile protection for the puppy. Through airport loading or unloading, a dog that can see out on top and all sides can be quickly scared by activity and sounds.

3. How to Choose a Puppy Pen

A puppy crate resembles a rigid-wire crate. It is usually square, with a wire roof, elevated bottom, and a removable pan if the puppy has an injury. These pens have much too much space for successful housebreaking, but they may help owners who must be away from home during training. They're about $200.

4. Crates Made of Collapsible Wire

Adjustable wire crates are identical to rigid-wire crates in terms of size and components, but they can be packed into a plain luggage box that is just six inches thick. An adjustable mesh crate can be folded and placed underneath a bed or even in a cupboard when not being used. These crates typically range in price from $90 to $175.

5. Crates Made of Soft Materials

You may choose to turn to a gentle style until your puppy is adequately crate conditioned and not violent in the crate. Soft crates are composed of a net composite made of synthetic or nylon and fiberglass rods. The crates have a curved roof and a plain bottom. They are tiny (a big one weighs just about 6 pounds) and fold up into a suitcase-like package around 6 inches thick.

A few ranges with shoulder straps and carrying cases, allowing you to take your dog while holding the crate on the other side. Crates made of soft materials will cost up to $150. As opposed to air transport crates, wire containers make the dog entirely vulnerable towards the outer world. They are ideal for the household where the dog can love watching what is going on. For days where the puppy would like more anonymity, they should be covered with a blanket. Soft crates are also available in tent-like designs.

They're deftly referred to as "pup tents," and they're made of durable cloth and fiberglass sticks. The design is comparable to that of a standard tent. Pup tents are available for measurements ranging from 33x33 inches. The medium-sized tent weighs around 2 pounds and fits nicely into a 5-inch-diameter bag. Soft crates or tents are not suggested for raising dogs or puppies and can never be used by dogs who dig, chew, or tear. Airlines do not allow soft crates for dogs traveling in the freight area. On the other hand, some airlines would allow a soft crate in the passenger compartment if it fit underneath the seats at the front of the traveler and the crate volume is sufficient for the dog.

6. Fold Up an Aluminum Crate

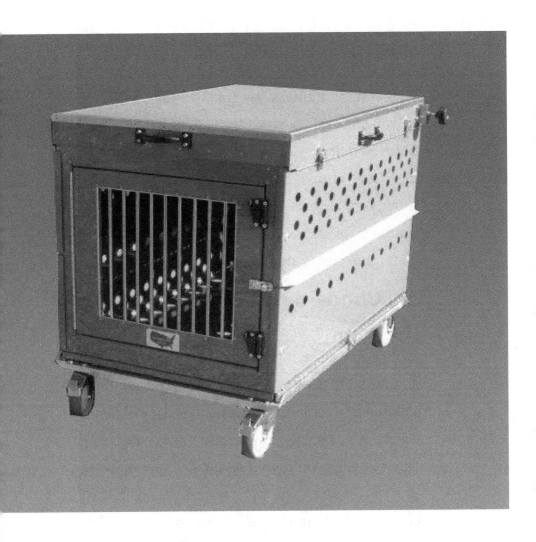

The thick, upright metal bars that make up the fold-up aluminum crate fold to a thickness of around 10 inches. It has a sturdy roof that can be used as a working table, and it has a wheel on the bottom.

This crate is more costly than a rigid-wire crate and an air transport crate, costing two to four times as much as a typically adjustable crate with the same volume. However, whether you want to show your dog or need them to be crated and compact for some other purpose, these fold-up aluminum crates are ideal.

2.5 Choosing a Perfect Crate for the Dog

A variety of factors decide the kind of crate suitable for the pup. Of course, the cost will play a role in your choice—look around before deciding on a crate. It would help if you also remembered your dog's type, age, height, and behavior. Dog crates can be seen in retail shops and pet supplies stores, and on selling stores online. The wheeled folding aluminum crate often doubles as dressing tables. These crates are ideal for show dogs. Below are the three main criteria to remember when picking a crate:

- Dimensions

- Airflow

- Surface covering

- The Appropriate Measurements

The crate with an untrained puppy or dog should be sufficiently big enough for the puppy to turn around, stand up, and lay down peacefully. Your pet will ease themself at one side of the crate and lay down at another if it's much more significant. A significantly bigger crate should be considered for the dogs that are adequately house trained. If you come across a cheap rate that is too big for the untrained puppy, you might be able to divide off a portion and make sure it works. If you intend on getting a sized 500 crate for a 10-pound puppy that will grow to weigh 100 pounds, you would need to divide the crate before they are disciplined in not dirtying it. You might use a rigid-wire frame, cardboard box, or pieces of wood to make a shield.

1. Bring the Dog to the Store

When looking for a crate or other supplies, some pet shops allow owners to bring the dogs with them—allowing your dog to "try products before you purchase. It will assist you in making choices that you and your dog will both be satisfied with. The below are the standard sizes for air transport crates. (Wire crates closely follow this sizing scheme.) All other crates are normally labeled "little," "moderate," etc., though differences exist.

Requirements for Ventilation Dogs with narrow muzzles (e.g., Pekingese, pug, boxer) or long fur coats (For example, Saint Bernard, chow chow, Alaskan malamute) and also oversized dogs will benefit from a wire crate because it allows for optimum airflow.

2. Choosing a Crate

If you prefer a durable air transport crate but want more airflow than it offers, look for one with more vents in the rear panel or drill a couple of holes in the edges, top, and back with a giant drill machine. As temperature increases, the rest of the holes must be in the crate's top portion. Position the crate in a position with plenty of airflow on both sides.

3. Convenient Floor Coverings

Heavy-coated breeds, such as St. Bernard, benefit from the open airflow of wire crates. Since the dog may use most of their crate time napping, they should be at ease in a flat position. Blisters and swollen patches on the knees, knuckles, and buttocks may occur in dogs that often relax on a rough or hard surface. The rug or other discarded clothes on the crate's floor didn't help; they will make their way to the other side of the crate, where they will mount up and have less padding for the dog's weak pressure areas.

Give the dog a crate pad instead of a blanket. The mat must be able to be cleaned in a standard washing machine. Mats made of cedar shavings cannot be washed. Crate mats vary in price from approximately $20 through $50, depending on size and materials used for the cover and filling. If your puppy is still in the training progress, recommend purchasing two mats, so you'll have one on hand if your puppy has an accident in the crate. Spread a crate mat over the floor of the crate to make the canine warm and secure.

4. Purchasing a Second-Hand Crate

If you're trying to save money, keep an eye out for backyard or garage deals and classified advertisements in the newspapers. You will have a used crate for a fraction of the price, which would be a quarter part of what you will pay for new. If you are fortunate enough to get a used crate that is the right size for the puppy, inspect all movable pieces, such as latches and hinges, as these can be costly to repair.

Dismantle and adequately disinfect the used crates with a washing-up liquid and bleach. Ammonia-based cleaners should be avoided. Before reassembling and using the crate, carefully rinse it to clear any chlorine signs and then let it dry for many days.

2.6 Maintenance of Crate

The crate's utility can be extended if you keep it in excellent condition. To help in house training, and extend the crate's life, keep the dog, their crate, and the bedding tidy. Look for fleas and ticks routinely, disinfect and sanitize the crate and bedding regularly. Few dogs are allergic to specific washing powder, so make sure to wash everything properly. If your dog is muddy or filthy, don't put them in the crate, as it results in rust and bacteria growth, requiring more frequent sanitization.

Use a parasite treatment regimen approved by your doctor to keep the dog free of parasites. There are some excellent parasite-controlling drugs on the market that last for a month or more. (Unless the vet advises, don't use more than one parasite prevention measure at once.) Any flea/tick repellents will potentially kill the dog if used together. Once every month, use an environmentally benign oil to grease the hinge and latches. Wipe away the remaining oil to avoid the dog licking the area where the oil has been sprayed. Inspect all metallic parts for polish or coating oil to certain affected areas to avoid corrosion.

2.7 Choosing an Appropriate Crate Place

A dog desires to be a member of the family. Place the crate in the room with the max. Family interaction because the dog would be most relaxed there, particularly in initial days. The crate can be brought into your room at night. Moreover, choose a place with lots of fresh air. Be assured there are no heater or air-conditioning outlets near the crate, as they can cause the temperatures inside to fluctuate. Place the crate away from a door or even in a direction where the sunshine will fall on it at any time of day, increase the temperature internally.

Before you place the dog into the crate, give them a "trial run": keep a thermometer within the crate and evaluate it many times over 24 hours. Dogs like to be at the center of family life, so the dog's crate must be around other family members, and you spend much of their time. A crate can be used as both a sanctuary for the dog and a dining table in the living room.

2.8 Crate Training the Pup

The critical aim of crate training is to teach your dog to enjoy their crate. The bulk of puppies are unafraid of the crate because they associate this with the comforting coziness of sleep time. However, don't push the dog to go into their crate if they don't want to. It will be a waste of time. Instead, use the activities below to teach them to enjoy it.

Consider this: It's better to do such a training exercise before the pup eats so that the treats you'll throw outside (and gradually inside) the crate can pique their interest.

1. Tossing Treats Around the Crate

Throw a few treats across the crate and heading towards the crate opening, then step back. After this, don't throw any treats into the crate. Say "nice" and throw a few more treats around the crate's opening if the pup looks at you and then the crate in which the treats were. (Have a plentiful stock in hand.)

When they are done with all of those rewards and turn to you further, back away and put a couple just inside the door. Throw the rewards a little further into the crate gradually. Keep quiet during such initial trials other than applaud the dog for expressing some involvement in the crate, such as smelling around it, approaching it, or attempting to enter it. Don't even use phrases like "inside your crate" or other vocal cues. If you lean down or take a step ahead, the dog can get anxious and feel trapped, making them afraid of the crate.

2. Load It with Treats

If your dog is still terrified of the crate, as some rescued dogs are, take it gradually and do several trials throwing rewards across the crate—you will have to feed them a complete meal out of the crate initially. To help them gain confidence heading into the open crate, open up the door and load it with treats, but don't push them. Encourage the dog to eat just out of the crate, just next to the entrance door. Ensure the crate gate is fastened so it doesn't swing open and frighten pups when they approach it.

3. Feed Portioned Meal in the Crate

As your dog is confident enough going in the crate, feed the portion of their food in a crate dish. As you'll be doing the hand-feeding method at the moment, use your better judgment while deciding how much pup can consume from a dish despite you touching the dog. When you've been spoon-feeding the dog in various rooms and using multiple dishes, they'll be more inclined to trust that going into the crate to chow down is secure. Behavior conditioning is a methodology you'll use to educate the dog on various training signals by making simple, gradual progress. You also can begin to acclimate your dog to eat in the crate by tossing a toy with a portion of their meal and placing it in there.

4. Feed Whole Meal in the Crate

The next move for your dog is to eat the whole meal inside. Put a chunk of the meal in a crate dish and walk away, having left the crate door wide open; afterward, you'll train your pup to concede getting fed with it closed. Crate Keep going to be quiet as they enter the crate to dine. Praise them when they finished the meal and turns to you for a refill. Try to serve them tiny portions of the remaining food. If they don't eat, they might not be prepared for this move, so take it slowly and ensure they will be hungry before proceeding. Don't push them; instead, praise them for what they do well and make a note in the teaching chart.

5. Naming the Crate

The crate's name would be the next move. Another method you can use to educate the signals is naming. Choose a title for the crate; we recommend something noticeable like "crib," "nap time," or "hut." Assume "nice crate" as you put a couple of snacks in it, and they go within it. You'll notice that you're not instructing anything new; instead, you're providing a title to something they are already performed. Consider making it an enjoyable game by chucking dog treats all around the crate approximately 10 times across the day.

The dog is picking up on the fact that excellent deeds take place there.

6. The Dog's Safe Zone Is the Crate

It's now time to train the dog to proceed on cues. A cue is a phrase or gesture that tells the dog what you'd like them to do. Begin from outside the crate with them. Allow them to see you putting some rewards in before closing the door. Say "crate" as you open the door. Say "nice crate" and lock the door as they enter. When the dog is inside, give them a few treats and applaud through the crate. Take a few moments before releasing them.

Say "nice crate" whether they sit in the crate or move outside and back again. When they exit, compliment them and shut the door, using the words "nice crate." Nearly seven times during the day, perform this process. If you find the activity interesting for the dog, they may want to do it more, which is incredible.

After that, keep a few rewards in your palm for your dog to sniff; don't place them in the crate. Open the crate, say "crate," and if they enter, give them the treats and compliment. Repeat this process 7 times more. Return to the previous stage if they don't understand or refuse.

7. Spend Time in the Crate

The next move is to encourage them to spend more time within the crate with the gate shut. Begin by demonstrating to the dog that you are placing some of the food in the dish. Taking the bowl in the side, unlock the gates and say "crate," then say "nice crate" and place the dish inside. Place a tiny amount of the food in a Kong (loaded with a rare treat, such as peanut butter) and put it in the food dish.

Shut the door gently as they continue to eat while repeating the word "nice crate." Please wait a few moments before opening the door after they end the portion of the food, and compliment them for being in the crate peacefully, so they know it's safe. When they come out, say "nice crate," and then fill the dish or Kong with more peanut butter. Load the Kong or food dish in front of them, so they understand you're the one that offers each of these great items, and then place the bowl in the crate. Lock the door as they go inside and enjoy food. Please wait a moment after they are done, applaud them, and then let them out.

It is indeed essential that you behave as if letting them out of the crate isn't a huge deal: no elation, no relaxation, just an incredible welcome and appreciation. After that, tell them to enter the crate, shut the door for a moment, and offer them the reward for an opening while praising them and calling the crate name. After this, unlock the gates to let them out, compliment them, call the crate name again as they walk out, and then shut the door behind them. It's better if they like to stay in the crate because they learned the system: great things come within the crate! Repeat this practice seven times more, every time leaving them in the locked crate for an extra second. (You'll finally incorporate other signals to crate training, such as settle, off, sit, down.)

8. Stay in Crate

Next begins the challenging part: Training the dog to stay in the crate when busy with some house tasks. Begin by making the dog observe you taking a step back while placing a reward by the closed-door while inside the crate., After this, come back, wait for a few moments, and remind them in a low, gentle tone that you are a good dog. Repeat the procedure with a special reward (such as a slice of hard cheese) inserted in the crate.

Take a step back and face away. Come back and wait for a few moments before releasing them. Repeat the process; make sure this time give a squeaky toy or a Kong to chew on while staying in the crate. Each time, increase the count of steps you take. While you increase time to repeat, bring some activity in the premises that they can see you doing, even though it's just shuffling files, lifting a box, relaxing down and watching a little Video, or making their food ready. Remember to consider letting the dog out of the crate as a regular, almost dull activity. The point is to ensure the dog that anytime you leave the premises, and they get something special in the crate.

9. Associate the Dog's Crate with Good Memories and Incentives

The last step in crate training is to leave the room. Most dogs may consider this move without hesitation immediately, while some will take several weeks. Never push the dog to advance quicker than their ability, or you may increase their stress and cause them to fall behind in the learning. Begin by going for a split second, entering, and releasing them.

With repetition, lengthen the time you spend on it. Offer the dog a Kong loaded with cookies or peanut butter as you perform these very last activities. Exit the room for a couple of seconds longer after each repeat. The intention is for the dog to get so caught up in Kong that they don't know you're going.

Walk into a nearby room and do something so the dog can notice, periodically attempting to enter to look over them and encourage, then exit. When the dog is used to it, continue putting them in the crate whenever you are out of the house. Initially, try to leave as quickly as possible. Last outside for a few moments and rejoin with some noise (but not too much). As a result, you will gradually increase the time of your absence and make it a bit sounder as you depart. Go out and do a brief, odd job at some point.

When you leave their sight, certain dogs will scream or bark in their crates. If this happens, don't show up again while making a racket since you may not want to assume that crying gets them anything (your existence). Stay, once they calm down and cease whining, then arrive back peacefully. Have a note in your record book of how long it took them to start whining, so the next time you do the same workout, you should be sure to return sooner, before they have an opportunity to start. When the dog whines or barks or for an extended period, you can go to a therapist or ethologist to see if it's the start of real anxiety issues or just part of the acclimating to their new place. Getting the dog charged up to the point that they start screaming and whining is detrimental.

Suppose the dog is nervous when you enter, or there are indications that they were distressed while you were out (their pillow is torn, for instance). In that case, you can ask some other individual; your dog likes to be in the room when you do these activities and then gradually exclude that individual. Changing the dog's enclosure to various rooms is indeed a smart move.

If the dog's behavior reverts at some point throughout this training session, you can stick to the crate drills. It isn't a form of retaliation. Instead, it's just a strategy for refocusing them on achievement.

Chapter 3: Weekend Plan for Crate Training

Most instructors and ethologist consider progressively moving the dog to a different crate after 1 week or 2. This technique is ideal for shy dogs afraid of being confined and puppies that have already developed a disdain for crates. However, most dogs may adapt to using crates more quickly, and many owners don't have the patience to dedicate a week or more to preparation until their dog can use them.

Consider the weekend crate-training schedule if you want the dog to practice using a crate as quickly as possible. On Monday, once the Saturday and Sunday practice sessions over, you'll be ready to initiate constraining the dog to the crate.

To attempt this crate-training session effectively, execute the guidelines below bit by bit. It's essential not to rush anything and leave the dog alone in the crate until ready. Better constrain the dog in a tiny, secure place at night on the weekend—cordon off a section of the kitchen, toilet, or laundry area with a baby gate or a training pen. Be assured the room is dog-proof and cleared of something the dog must not bite on. To get them entertained, provide them with a comfortable place to lay down, some water, several toys, and some chewable items. It's advisable to never keep the dog alone in-home on weekends throughout the day. If you need to leave the house for whatever reason, you should do so in that same dog-proof environment to stay on track for the training.

3.1 Getting Started by Selecting a Crate

Metal crates, plastic flight crates, and net crates are available from pet supplies shops and online retailers. Every style would have its own set of benefits. Metal crates probably appear for space and functionality, and they have better airflow than plastic crates. Plastic crates have a nest appearance that can help dogs feel better and much more comfortable inside. Net crates are by far the most compact and have anonymity for puppies, but they're not very sturdy. Usually, dogs bite on them and manage to get free.

1. Comfortable Crate

It's critical to keep the crate cozy after deciding which type of crate to buy. It should be in a place where you spend countless hours, but apart from pedestrian traffic. Place a comfortable mattress or rug inside, along with few toys. You can even place a top that you've just wear so that the dog can smell you. (You can omit this step if the dog enjoys chewing on cloth.) If you buy your puppy a wire crate, they may prefer to have a sheet or towels thrown around it to make it feel somewhat "sanctuary."

3.2 When You Begin Coaching: Friday Night

Crate teaching is more successful when the dog connects their crate to objects they love. To persuade the dog to stay in the new crate, consider the following suggestions:

1. Fairy of Treats

Be assured your dog has exposure to space where the crate is installed while keeping the crate gate open. When dogs aren't focused, throw a few rewards across and into the crate to find them independently. Small bits of meat, cheese, sausage, or thaw liver are good choices for the dog. You may also cram a plush Kong doll inside the crate or an interesting new toy, a tasty chew item; keep spare rewards in the puppy's crate every night for the coming few weeks. When your dog discovers unexpected treats in the crate occasionally, they will develop a fondness for it and frequently enter it to check whether the "Treat Fairy" has arrived.

2. Services in Room

Place the dog's bowl within the crate and open the door when it's time for them to feed. Consider placing the dish in the crate's rear side so that the dog could feed when standing in. When they decline to enter the crate initially, place the dish just near the door. They'll just have to put their head in the crate in this manner. It would help if you eventually kept the dish to the other side of the crate and shut the crate gate while the dog enjoys the meals as they get more relaxed moving inside.

3. Prepare for Saturdays and Sundays with the Requisite Supplies

You must praise the dog for entering the crate several times during the next few days. Preparing few snacks beforehand so is a wise choice. Set aside some meat, cheese, sausages, fluffy dog food, or thaw liver in bite-sized bits for future use. You could also stuff a few KONGs that the puppy offers while you continue to lengthen the crate duration.

3.3 Let the Crate Games Begin! Saturday Morning

You are now prepared to start. Bring your dog to the crate with the rewards you made earlier.

Stage 1: Adhere to the Plan

The following exercises should be performed either seated on the ground or in a chair beside the crate.

Give your dog a cue, like "Go to sleep," to ask them to enter the crate. (You can use any cue you want; just make sure you have been using the same one every time.) Offer one reward to the dog and throw it into the crate. When they enter inside to enjoy it, heap praise on them and feed some other reward while already inside, say "OK, so that dog understands they may step out again," you shouldn't have to give them anything when they get out of the crate. They are required to realize that everything positive happens within the crate.

Repeat the previous measures 10 times more. After a quick break (for some minutes), execute a further sequence of 10 attempts. Finish the workout after this practice.

Stage 2: Obtain the Reward

Grab few snacks late morning and take the dog to the crate for further exercise. Attempt to encourage them to go inside the crate before enticing them with the treat since they have gotten the hang of it.

Warm-up by tossing the snack into the crate and letting the dog pursue it for a few repetitions, much as you practiced before. The regulations can then be tweaked a bit.

Instead of tossing a reward into the crate, give the cue, "Go to rest," and nod to it. (While aiming, raise the hand in the very same way that you did when throwing a reward into the crate.) The recognizable gesture will make the dog understand what they ought to do.

When the dog enters the crate, applaud them and offer a handful of rewards while they already in there.

Say "All right," and bring the dog out of the crate.

After 10 attempts, take a brief rest. Repeat the task ten times more, or unless the dog appears to understand the activity and exits and enters with no trouble as you demand. Suppose the dog is worried about getting into the crate or is unclear what they should do once you give the signal; go back to the previous step and try it again. Step 2 should be repeated until the dog happily rushes into the crate to get the reward.

3.4 Shut the Crate Door Saturday Afternoon

It's now appropriate to acclimate the dog to continue in the crate with the doors locked.

Perform several repetitions as you did before to warm it up. Say "Go to rest," refer to the crate, give the dog a treat as they enter, and afterward say "All right" to let them out.

Now try shutting the crate door for a few seconds. Say "Go to rest," referring to the crate.

Appreciate the dog and give them a treat as soon as they enter the crate. Then shut the crate gate softly. (At this stage, you don't have to lock it.) Offer the dog 3 or 4 treats through the crate gate that is locked, and compliment them as they are inside. Tell 'alright' and ask them to come out of the crate. (If the dog is anxious or frightened when the gate is just partially closed, divide the exercise into 2 stages: first, close the door partially, offer a reward, and free the dog; in the next stage, shut the door completely.)

Conduct 10 attempts and then take a couple of minutes to rest. Then perform the procedure ten times again, gradually increasing the amount of time the dog spends in the crate with the door shut. Have some fast repetitions while you lengthen the time. Begin with 1 second and work your way up to 5. Attempt 8 seconds, then return to 3 seconds. Boost to 10 seconds, eventually 15, 20, and finally a simple 5. When the dog is in the crate, proceed to praise them lavishly—taking a slight break after completing the second sequence of 10 attempts. Then go through the practice some more. Try to get the dog to sit in the crate for a minute throughout the day.

3.5 Introduction of Alone Time on a Saturday Evening

When the dog feels secure in their crate while the door shut and you are around, then you may proceed to the further stage, letting them alone for a brief amount of time. Continue the activity you've been doing, but this time bolt the crate gate and begin moving away from the crate, as outlined above.

Conduct a couple of attempts, as you were doing in the daytime, to warm up. Besides your dog's crate, sit on the ground or even on a chair. Tell "Go to rest," referring to the crate. Lock the crate door once the dog enters and treat them with a few snacks while remaining in the crate— Approx. after 30 seconds. Tell "Alright," and unlock the crate door and ask the dog to come out. It would help if you locked the crate gate for a few moments. Tell the cue "Go to rest," referring to the crate. Close and bolt the crate door once the dog enters and afterward reward them.

Take a step forward and give the dog some treat. Return to the crate after a few moves out to reward the dog. Tell "All right," and then unlock the crate door and allow the dog to come out. Repeat the previous measures 10 times more, every time going away in different ways. Conduct 10 more attempts after a slight respite, gradually increasing the amount of time your dog sits in the crate as you move across the room.

Add some quick repetitions while you increase the amount of time. Initiate with 10 seconds and work your way up to 15. Target 20 seconds, then return to 10 seconds. Boost to 30 seconds, then to 15, then to 45, and eventually to a quick 5. While your dog is within the crate, keep coming back to it and rewarding them after a few seconds. Be very charitable initially. You will eventually reduce how much you treat the dog as they seem more relaxed staying in the crate.

Have a slight break after finishing the second sequence of 10 attempts. Now again, continue the exercise ten times again. Begin by leaving the room for several seconds, entering to praise the dog while still in the crate. Step your way back up to letting your dog remain in the crate for a couple of minutes as you pace across the room and exit the room momentarily.

3.6 Sunday Morning: It's Television Day

You'll train your dog to rest in the crate for extended periods this morning. You'll need to have some snacks, a nice tasty chewing bone, or a Kong loaded with anything good, either cream cheese or peanut butter, as well as a toy to keep the dog entertained. Instruct the puppy to enter the crate. Admire them and offer the chewing bone or Kong once she succeeds. Again, lock the crate door and relax in the same area to listen to music or watch a movie.

For almost 30 minutes, leave the dog in the crate. (As much as they remain calm, you can occasionally give them a treat if they finish the chew.) Once the half-hour is over, unlock the crate gently and say "Alright" to let your dog out. Remove the chew toy and don't offer the treats once the crate period comes to an end. It's preferable if you forget the dog for a couple of minutes. It would be best to understand that beautiful things are happening in the crate instead of getting out. For a moment, take a rest from practicing. You should replicate the activity an hour later.

1. Complaining Dogs

Your dog could begin to protest to being restricted in the crate at this phase in the learning. You have two choices whether they bark or whines:

Ignore them. (If appropriate, grab a pair of earbuds.) Don't surrender to the shouting when the dog is trying to grab your attention. Pretend they aren't there. You may give them a treat as soon as they finish barking for a couple of seconds. Your puppy will understand that they might be avoided if it gets louder, but they will be rewarded with delicious treats once they are calm.

Give a gesture with some noise to realize the dog, and they made a mess up as soon as they start barking or whining. You must walk out of the room right after saying "Ouch!" or "Really terrible." Come back after the dog has been silent for about 5 to 10 seconds. Your dog may eventually discover that yelling causes you to exit right away, but being calm causes you to return.

So, if your dog shouts in the crate, you must act accordingly as above. It can be challenging initially, but if you adhere to the schedule, they'll understand that resting peacefully in the crate is the most significant advantage.

3.7 Alone Time on a Sunday Afternoon

Give the dog proper exercise before going on to Sunday afternoon workouts. Take them for a fast stroll or sprint outdoors, play catch or tug with them, or let them interact with a dog friend. When they are exhausted, crate handling would be smoother. Reiterate the training procedure you practiced this morning once you've walked your puppy; at that time, instead of sitting in the same space as the dog, and you'll walk around the home. Instruct the puppy to enter the crate.

Give a tasty chewing bone or a loaded Kong while they go inside. Then exit the room by closing the crate flap. Stay away from the room for ten minutes. You should return and release the dog out from the crate once the timer has elapsed. (If they haven't stopped chewing on the chew toy by the time it exits the crate, remove it.) Through crate period, they deserve special treats. If the dog gets louder in the crate when you're out, wait for 10 to 15 seconds before returning to let them out. Repeat these steps after a small rest. Continue to perpetuate the moves above this afternoon, steadily increasing the amount of time the dog spends in the crate. Work your way close to an hour, some alone time.

3.8 It's Time to Get Out of the House on Sunday Evening

You're prepared to leave the dog alone in the home so they can comfortably sit in the crate for an hour as you walk around the house. Like, tell the dog to go into the crate and offer some tasty item to chew or consume. Then lock the crate and go outside for around ten minutes without bowing down. Once you come back, kindly free your dog from the crate and remove the chew toy. Refrain from partying. When you behave as if getting into or out of the crate isn't something out of this world, the dog becomes more at ease.

Repeat the routine as many times as possible until going to bed, having a break for workouts, and pee breaks in between. Eventually, you must be able to leave the dog alone in the crate for a couple of hours.

3.9 The Weekend Has Come to an End. So, What Will Be Next?

After executing the Weekend Crate-Training schedule, your dog will begin to sit in the crate if you leave home, night time, even when you cannot oversee them throughout the day. Ignore the crate period instructions earlier and follow the previous recommendations in mind to keep your dog secure in the crate.

Sometimes, make sure to give the dog a decent workout before putting them in a crate. (minimum 30 to 60 minutes of aerobic activity is recommended.) If you crate the dog when you are at the job and nighttime, they'll need plenty of quality play sessions and workouts while they're not in the crate. Until crating the dog and right after getting them free from the crate, please take them out for a pee break. Keep feeding the dog food within the crate to make sure the dog has plenty to bite on when the dog is around. (If you're not aware of what your dog will chew once dogs are alone, contact your veterinarian.)

If you save special treats for crate time, such as supper, different chewing bones, loaded Kong, and ears of the pig, your dog can come to enjoy it. Try to keep the dog's crate unlocked at all hours so they can get into the crate. And if they wouldn't have to, several dogs like to sleep in their crates.

Conclusion

Training a puppy with love and consistency is the basis for a peaceful and stress-free coexistence between humans and dogs. The fact that the dog understands from the beginning what their place is within the family and where the limits are will not only help to create a pleasant atmosphere in the home but also to develop healthily.

The dog is an animal accustomed to living in a pack, which requires rules and routines to feel good psychologically. A careless or insecure owner who gives excessive freedom or behaves inconsistently confuses the animal and can trigger unwanted or even dangerous behaviors, which will be more difficult to modify the more time passes.

CPSIA information can be obtained
at www.ICGtesting.com
Printed in the USA
LVHW081021110621
689237LV00041B/568